THE KITCHEN LIBRARY
SALADS

D0339115

THE KITCHEN LIBRARY
SALADS

Carole Handslip

OCTOPUS BOOKS

CONTENTS

This edition published 1989 by
Octopus Books Limited
a division of the Octopus Publishing Group
Michelin House
81 Fulham Road
London SW3 6RB

© Cathay Books 1984
ISBN 0 7064 3840 X

Printed by Mandarin Offset in Hong Kong

INTRODUCTION

Salads – served as main courses, starters or accompaniments – are nutritious, colourful, refreshing and usually quick and easy to prepare. They provide valuable minerals, vitamins and fibre in the diet, and are mostly low in calories.

Salads need not only be eaten in summer months when there is a wonderful selection of vegetables available; we need their health-giving properties even more in winter. Although it is possible to buy most summer salad ingredients all year round, they are more expensive out of season and often less flavoursome. In winter months use vegetables that are at their best at this time of year, such as beetroot, Jerusalem artichokes, carrots and white cabbage.

Thoughtful selection of ingredients is essential for the presentation of an appetising salad. Don't combine too many different ingredients or chop them into small pieces: this will produce a messy appearance, and flavour and texture will be lost.

Fresh herbs greatly enhance the flavour of salads so don't be afraid to use them liberally. Experiment by using a different herb each time you make a salad. Parsley, marjoram, thyme and chives are particularly useful as they go well with most salad ingredients and can also be added to dressings. Basil goes well with tomatoes, while fennel and dill are good with fish salads, beetroot and cucumber.

Many of these salads are suitable to serve as first courses or, accompanied by crusty bread or a garlic loaf, they can be served as a light lunch.

NOTES

Standard spoon measurements are used in all recipes
1 tablespoon = one 15 ml spoon
1 teaspoon   = one 5 ml spoon
All spoon measures are level.

Use freshly ground black pepper where pepper is specified.

Fresh herbs are used unless otherwise stated.

For all recipes, quantities are given in both metric and imperial measures. Follow either set but not a mixture of both, because they are not interchangeable.

Salad dressings are marked with an asterisk in the ingredients list. Recipes are given on pages 76–81.

SALAD STARTERS

Avocado in Soured Cream

Avocado pears must be eaten when their flesh is quite soft. To test for ripeness, cradle the fruit in the palm of your hand – it should yield to gentle pressure. Avocados can be stored in the refrigerator for up to 1 week. To hasten ripening, keep them in a fruit bowl with other fruit, such as apples. Once cut, avocados should be brushed with lemon juice to avoid discoloration.

4 avocado pears
150 ml (¼ pint)
Soured cream
dressing*
TO GARNISH:
watercress sprigs
3 tablespoons
lumpfish caviar
(optional)

Cut the avocado pears in half and remove the stones. Scoop out the flesh with a melon scoop or cut into cubes and place in a bowl; reserve the shells.

Pour the dressing over the avocado pieces. Toss well, then spoon back into 6 of the shells. Garnish with watercress and caviar, if using.

Serves 6

Avocado with Caviar

The most common type of avocado pear is characteristically pear-shaped with a speckled green skin. The distinctive Hass variety is similar in flavour but has a dark purple knobbly skin.

3 avocado pears
4 tablespoons French
   dressing*
3 tablespoons
   lumpfish caviar

Cut the avocado pears in half and remove the stones. Peel each half and lay, cut side down, on a board. Slice across thinly, then lift onto a serving plate and press firmly to separate the slices.

Add 1 tablespoon of the dressing to the caviar and mix well. Spoon the remaining dressing over the avocados to coat completely, then spoon the caviar down the centre of each pear. Serve immediately.

Serves 6

Asparagus Vinaigrette

500 g (1 lb)
  asparagus
salt
4 tablespoons Lemon
  vinaigrette
  dressing*
1 hard-boiled egg
1 tablespoon chopped
  parsley

Cut the asparagus stalks all the same length, tie in bundles and place upright in a deep pan of boiling salted water. Make a lid with foil and dome it over the tips so that the heads cook in the steam. Small asparagus will take 15 minutes to cook; large stems up to 30 minutes. Drain very carefully, then arrange on a serving dish and leave to cool.

Spoon the dressing over the asparagus. Chop the egg white finely and sprinkle over the asparagus. Sieve the egg yolk over the top and sprinkle with the parsley.

Serves 4

Palm Heart and Avocado Vinaigrette

few curly endive
  leaves
1 × 425 g (15 oz)
  can palm hearts,
  drained
1 avocado pear
3 tablespoons French
  dressing*
2 tablespoons sesame
  seeds, toasted

Tear the endive into pieces and arrange on 6 individual serving dishes. Cut the palm hearts into quarters lengthways. Cut the avocado pear in half and remove the stone. Peel each half and slice lengthwise. Arrange both on the endive, pour over the dressing and sprinkle with the sesame seeds.

Serves 6

Leeks Vinaigrette

8 thin leeks
salt
1 hard-boiled egg,
  finely chopped
1 tablespoon chopped
  parsley
4 tablespoons French
  dressing*
125 g (4 oz) streaky
  bacon, derinded
  and chopped

Trim the leeks, if necessary, to about 15 cm (6 inches); split lengthways as far as necessary to clean thoroughly.

Cook in boiling salted water for 8 minutes, until just tender. Drain well, arrange on individual serving dishes and leave to cool.

Add the egg and parsley to the dressing and spoon over the leeks. Fry the bacon in its own fat until crisp, then sprinkle over the leeks.

Serves 4

Gazpacho Ring

1 × 397 g (14 oz)
   can tomatoes
2 cloves garlic,
   chopped
150 ml (1/4 pint)
   water
1 bouquet garni
1/2–1 teaspoon sugar
salt and pepper
1 tablespoon gelatine,
   soaked in 4 table-
   spoons cold water
6 tablespoons French
   dressing*

SALAD:
4 tomatoes, skinned,
   seeded and diced
1/4 cucumber, diced
1/2 green pepper,
   cored, seeded and
   diced
1/2 onion, finely
   chopped

Place the tomatoes, with their juice, in a pan with the garlic, water and bouquet garni. Add sugar, salt and pepper to taste. Bring slowly to the boil, then simmer for 5 minutes. Discard the bouquet garni.

Place the mixture in an electric blender or food processor. Add the soaked gelatine and blend on maximum speed for 30 seconds. Leave to cool.

Add 4 tablespoons of the dressing and half the salad ingredients and stir well. Turn into a 750 ml (1¼ pint) non-stick ring mould and chill in the refrigerator for about 3 hours, or until set.

Mix the remaining salad ingredients with the remaining French dressing. Turn out the tomato ring onto a serving plate and place the salad in the centre.
Serves 6

10

Crudités with Aïoli

Aïoli is a Provençal dish. It should be very thick and smooth, with a powerful garlic flavour. Any combination of salad vegetables can be served as crudités; other possibilities are radishes, cucumber, courgettes and fennel.

½ small cauliflower
4 carrots
4 celery sticks
1 green and 1 red pepper, cored and seeded
250 g (8 oz) baby new potatoes, boiled
AIOLI:
2 egg yolks
6 cloves garlic, crushed
½ teaspoon salt
300 ml (½ pint) olive oil
1–2 teaspoons lemon juice

Break the cauliflower into florets and cut the carrots, celery and peppers into matchstick pieces.

To make the aïoli, beat the egg yolks with the garlic and salt to thicken. Add the oil drop by drop, beating constantly. As it thickens, add 1 teaspoon lemon juice, then add the oil in a steady stream, beating vigorously. Add the remaining lemon juice to taste and mix thoroughly.

Turn the aïoli into a small bowl, place on a large plate and surround with the vegetables.

Serves 4

NOTE: If tiny new carrots are available, they are perfect used whole.

Frisée aux Lardons

3 slices bread, crusts
    removed
4 tablespoons oil
125 g (4 oz) streaky
    bacon, sliced 5 mm
    (¼ inch) thick
½ head curly endive
6 tablespoons
    Vinaigrette
    dressing*
3 hard-boiled eggs,
    sliced

Cut the bread into 5 mm (¼ inch)
cubes. Heat the oil in a pan, add the
bread cubes and fry until golden;
drain on kitchen paper.

Cut the bacon into 5 mm (¼ inch)
strips, add to the pan and fry until
golden brown.

Tear the endive into pieces and
place in a salad bowl. Pour over half
the vinaigrette dressing and toss well.
Arrange the eggs in a circle on top,
leaving a border of endive.

Place the croûtons in the centre and
sprinkle with the bacon. Pour over
the remaining dressing just before
serving.
Serves 4 to 6

Melon, Tomato and Kiwi Vinaigrette

This is a delicious light, refreshing starter – ideal for a warm summer's day. If kiwi fruit is unobtainable, use ¼ cucumber, diced, instead.

2 Ogen or Charentais melons
4 tomatoes, skinned
3 kiwi fruit, peeled and sliced
1 tablespoon chopped mixed herbs (e.g. chives, mint, parsley)
4 tablespoons Honey and lemon dressing*
2 tablespoons pumpkin seeds (optional)

Cut the melons in half and discard the seeds. Scoop the flesh into balls, using a melon baller, or cut into cubes; reserve the shells. Cut each tomato into 8 wedges and discard the seeds.

Place the melon in a bowl with the tomatoes, kiwi fruit and herbs. Pour over the dressing and toss well.

Spoon the mixture into the melon shells and sprinkle with pumpkin seeds if using, to serve.

Serves 4

NOTE: Pumpkin seeds are available from healthfood stores.

Peperonata

2 large red peppers
2 large green peppers
4 tablespoons olive oil
1 onion, sliced
2 cloves garlic,
  crushed
4 tomatoes, skinned,
  seeded and
  shredded
salt and pepper

Halve the peppers, discard the cores and seeds, and slice thinly. Heat the oil in a pan, add the onion and fry for 5 minutes, until softened. Add the garlic and peppers, cover and cook gently for 10 to 15 minutes, stirring occasionally.

Add the tomatoes, and salt and pepper to taste. Cook for a further 10 minutes, stirring occasionally. Leave to cool. Serve in individual dishes.
Serves 6

Aubergine Salad

2 aubergines
salt and pepper
4 tablespoons olive oil
1 onion, chopped
2 cloves garlic, finely
  chopped
4 tomatoes, skinned,
  seeded and chopped
2 tablespoons
  chopped parsley
1 tablespoon lemon
  juice
few lettuce leaves

Cut the aubergines into 1 cm (½ inch) cubes. Place in a colander, sprinkle with salt and leave for 30 minutes. Rinse and dry with kitchen paper.

Heat the oil in a frying pan, add the onion and aubergine and fry for 10 to 15 minutes, stirring occasionally, until golden. Add the garlic and tomatoes and fry for 2 to 3 minutes.

Leave to cool, then mix with the parsley, lemon juice, and pepper to taste. Arrange the lettuce leaves in a serving dish and spoon the salad into the centre.
Serves 4 to 6

Ratatouille Salad

6 tablespoons olive oil
1 small aubergine,
  sliced
250 g (8 oz)
  courgettes, sliced
1 green pepper,
  cored, seeded and
  sliced
2 cloves garlic,
  crushed
salt and pepper
4 tomatoes, skinned
  and sliced

Heat half the oil in a frying pan, add the aubergine and fry on both sides until light golden brown, adding more oil if necessary. Place in a salad bowl.

Add the remaining oil to the pan and fry the courgettes and pepper for 8 to 10 minutes, stirring occasionally, until softened. Add the garlic, and salt and pepper to taste and fry for 2 minutes. Add to the aubergines with the tomatoes and toss thoroughly. Cool before serving.
Serves 4 to 6

Tomato and Anchovy Salad

4 hard-boiled eggs
1 tablespoon capers
2 tablespoons
    chopped gherkins
6 tomatoes, skinned
    and halved
DRESSING:
4 tablespoons French
    dressing*
2 tablespoons tomato
    ketchup
2 tablespoons
    chopped mixed
    herbs

TO GARNISH:
1 × 50 g (1¾ oz) can
    anchovies, drained
watercress sprigs

Slice the hard-boiled eggs and arrange them in 4 individual shallow dishes. Sprinkle with the capers and gherkins. Place 3 tomato halves, cut side down, on each dish.

Place the dressing ingredients in a small bowl and mix together thoroughly. Spoon over the tomatoes to cover completely.

Split the anchovies lengthways into 2, or 3 if very thick, and arrange in a cross on top of each tomato. Garnish with watercress to serve.

Serves 4

Caponata

A traditional Sicilian dish which can be served as a main course accompanied by crusty bread.

1 large aubergine
salt and pepper
2 celery sticks, diced
3 tablespoons olive
    oil
1 onion, chopped
1 × 227 g (8 oz) can
    tomatoes, drained
    and chopped
1½ teaspoons tomato
    purée
40 g (1½ oz) green
    olives, stoned
1 tablespoon wine
    vinegar
1½ teaspoons soft
    brown sugar
1 tablespoon capers
few lettuce leaves

Cut the aubergine into 1 cm (½ inch) cubes. Place in a colander, sprinkle with salt and leave for 30 minutes. Rinse and dry with kitchen paper.

Blanch the celery in boiling water for 5 minutes; drain.

Heat 2 tablespoons of the oil in a heavy-based pan, add the aubergines and fry for 10 to 15 minutes, stirring frequently, until beginning to turn golden. Remove from the pan.

Add the remaining oil to the pan and fry the onion gently for 5 minutes, until softened. Add the tomatoes, tomato purée, olives, celery, and salt and pepper to taste. Cover and simmer for 5 minutes.

Add the vinegar, sugar, capers and aubergine, cover and simmer for 5 minutes; leave to cool. Serve on individual dishes lined with the lettuce leaves.

Serves 4 to 5

Herring and Apple Salad

2 rollmops
few curly endive
    leaves
2 red-skinned apples,
    cored
1 small onion, thinly
    sliced
150 ml (¼ pint)
    Soured cream
    dressing*
ground paprika

Open out the rollmops, cut in half lengthways, then into 1 cm (½ inch) pieces.

Arrange the endive on individual serving dishes. Slice the apple thinly into rings.

Arrange the rollmops, apples and onion in layers over the endive. Coat with the dressing and sprinkle with paprika to taste.
Serves 4

LEAFY VEGETABLE SALADS

Endive, chicory, spinach, cabbage, Chinese leaves, lamb's lettuce (corn salad) and dandelion all provide interesting alternatives to lettuce in salads.

To store leafy vegetables for short periods, wrap them in a polythene bag and keep them in the salad compartment of the refrigerator. Watercress is best kept with the leaves completely immersed in a bowl of water.

Avoid cutting leafy vegetables with a knife because this breaks the plant cells and releases an enzyme which destroys the vitamin C. Always tear leaves by hand to keep this loss to a minimum.

Broccoli and Almond Salad

350 g (12 oz) broccoli
salt
50 g (2 oz) split
    almonds, toasted
1 small red pepper,
    cored, seeded and
    thinly sliced
4 tablespoons
    Vinaigrette
    dressing*

Break the broccoli into florets and blanch in boiling salted water for 4 minutes. Drain and leave to cool.

Place in a salad bowl with the almonds and red pepper. Pour over the dressing and toss thoroughly.
Serves 4 to 6

Spinach and Onion Salad

750 g (1½ lb)
   spinach
2 tablespoons olive
   oil
1 large onion,
   chopped
2 cloves garlic,
   crushed
salt and pepper
142 ml (5 fl oz)
   single cream
grated nutmeg

Cook the spinach in a large pan, with just the water clinging to the leaves after washing, for 5 minutes. Drain thoroughly and chop.

Heat the oil in a pan, add the onion and fry until softened. Add the garlic, spinach, and salt and pepper to taste and heat through.

Season the cream to taste with nutmeg and pepper. Pour over the spinach and mix well. Leave to cool, then transfer to a salad bowl.

Serves 4

Salade de Pissenlits

125 g (4 oz)
    dandelion leaves
2 hard-boiled eggs,
    chopped
125 g (4 oz) streaky
    bacon, derinded
    and chopped
1 clove garlic, crushed
2 tablespoons cider
    vinegar
pepper

Trim the dandelion leaves, wash them well and dry thoroughly. Place in a salad bowl with the eggs.

Fry the bacon in its own fat until golden, then add the garlic and fry until the bacon is crisp. Pour the hot bacon and fat over the dandelion leaves and toss well.

Add the cider vinegar to the pan, stir to dissolve any juices and pour over the salad. Add plenty of pepper and toss thoroughly.

Serves 4

NOTE: Pick pale-coloured dandelion leaves; to make them less bitter, cover them with a bucket for a few days. Spinach can be used as a substitute.

Spring Green Salad

250 g (8 oz) spring
    greens
4 tablespoons olive
    oil
2 teaspoons soy sauce
1 tablespoon lemon
    juice
2 cloves garlic,
    crushed
salt and pepper
3 celery sticks
½ × 198 g (7 oz) can
    sweetcorn, drained
2 tablespoons
    chopped parsley

Shred the spring greens finely and place in a mixing bowl. Mix together the oil, soy sauce, lemon juice, garlic, and salt and pepper to taste and pour over the greens. Mix thoroughly and leave to marinate for 1 hour.

Slice the celery and add to the salad with the sweetcorn and parsley. Mix thoroughly, then transfer to a serving dish.

Serves 6

Spinach and Roquefort Salad

250 g (8 oz) young
    spinach leaves
50 g (2 oz) walnuts,
    roughly chopped
250 ml (8 fl oz)
    Roquefort
    dressing*

Trim the stalks from the spinach, wash and dry thoroughly, then tear into pieces. Place in a salad bowl with the walnuts and pour over the dressing. Toss thoroughly before serving.

Serves 6

Chinese Salad

2.5 cm (1 inch) piece
  root ginger, finely
  chopped
4 tablespoons French
  dressing*
1 Chinese cabbage
½ cucumber
125 g (4 oz)
  beanshoots
6 spring onions,
  chopped
1 tablespoon chopped
  parsley, to garnish

Mix the ginger with the dressing and leave for 30 minutes. Shred the Chinese cabbage and cut the cucumber into julienne strips. Place all the ingredients in a bowl and toss thoroughly to combine with the dressing. Transfer to a serving dish and sprinkle with the parsley.
Serves 6

Red Cabbage and Apple Salad

350 g (12 oz) red
  cabbage
1 small leek
6 tablespoons
  Vinaigrette
  dressing*
3 dessert apples,
  quartered and cored

Finely shred the cabbage, and thinly slice the leek. Place in a salad bowl, add the dressing and toss thoroughly. Leave to marinate for 1 hour, tossing occasionally.
  Slice the apples thinly. Add to the bowl and toss again just before serving.
Serves 8

Red Salad

250 g (8 oz) red
  cabbage
5 tablespoons Garlic
  dressing*
1 head of radicchio
1 small red onion
1 bunch of radishes

Finely shred the cabbage and place in a bowl with the dressing. Toss well and leave for 1 hour.

Separate the radicchio into leaves, then tear into pieces; thinly slice the onion and radishes. Add to the bowl and toss thoroughly, then transfer to a salad bowl.
Serves 6 to 8

Chinese Cabbage and Pepper Salad

1 leek, finely sliced
1 Chinese cabbage,
  shredded
1 green pepper,
  cored, seeded and
  finely sliced
6 tablespoons Herb
  dressing*

Separate the leek slices into rings and mix with the Chinese cabbage in a bowl. Add the green pepper and dressing and toss thoroughly. Transfer to a salad bowl and serve immediately.
Serves 6 to 8

Californian Coleslaw

1 dessert apple, cored
4 tablespoons Honey
    and lemon
    dressing*
2 oranges
125 g (4 oz) each
    white and black
    grapes, halved and
    seeded
250 g (8 oz) white
    cabbage, finely
    shredded
2 tablespoons
    chopped chives
2 tablespoons roasted
    sunflower seeds

Slice the apple thinly into the dressing and toss until thoroughly coated.

Remove the peel and pith from the oranges, break into segments and add to the bowl.

Add the remaining ingredients and toss well. Transfer to a salad bowl.
Serves 6 to 8

Caesar Salad

This salad was created by an Italian, Caesar Cardini, for his restaurant in Tihvana, Mexico. It subsequently acquired an international reputation.

2 cloves garlic,
    crushed
6 tablespoons olive
    oil
3 slices bread
2 tablespoons lemon
    juice
1 teaspoon Worcester-
    shire sauce
salt and pepper
1 large cos lettuce
2 eggs, boiled for
    1 minute
4 tablespoons grated
    Parmesan cheese

Place the garlic in the olive oil and leave to soak for 3 to 4 hours. Strain the oil.

Cut the bread into 5 mm (¼ inch) cubes and fry in 4 tablespoons of the garlic-flavoured oil until golden. Drain on kitchen paper.

Place the remaining oil in a small bowl with the lemon juice, Worcestershire sauce, and salt and pepper to taste and mix well.

Tear the lettuce into pieces and place in a salad bowl. Pour over the prepared dressing and toss well.

Break the eggs over the lettuce, scraping out the partly set egg white, and mix thoroughly to combine the egg with the dressing.

Add the cheese and croûtons and give a final toss just before serving.
Serves 6

Endive and Avocado Salad

½ head of curly
  endive
1 bunch of watercress
2 avocado pears,
  halved and stoned
6 tablespoons French
  dressing*

Tear the endive into pieces and
separate the watercress into sprigs;
place in a salad bowl.

Peel the avocados and slice into a
bowl. Pour over the dressing and toss
until completely coated. Add to the
endive and watercress and toss
thoroughly.
Serves 6

Chicory and Orange Salad

3 heads of chicory
3 oranges
1 tablespoon chopped
  parsley
4 tablespoons Honey
  and lemon
  dressing*

Cut the chicory diagonally across into
1 cm (½ inch) slices and place in a
salad bowl.

Remove the peel and pith from the
oranges and break into segments,
holding the fruit over the salad bowl
so that any juice is included.

Add the parsley and dressing and
toss thoroughly just before serving.
Serves 4

Watercress and Tofu Salad

Tofu is a soya bean curd with a soft delicate texture, sold in slabs. It is widely used in Chinese cooking, but is also good used in salads.

1 × 300 g (10 oz) cake of tofu
2 tablespoons sesame seeds, roasted
4 tablespoons Soy sauce dressing*
2 bunches of watercress

Cut the tofu into 1 cm (½ inch) cubes. Place in a bowl with the sesame seeds, pour over the dressing and toss carefully. Divide the watercress into sprigs, add to the tofu and mix gently. Transfer to a salad bowl.
Serves 4 to 6

Radicchio Salad

½ head of curly endive
1 head of radicchio
1 large head of chicory
4 tablespoons Lime vinaigrette dressing*
25 g (1 oz) pine nuts

Separate the endive and radicchio into leaves, tear into pieces and place in a bowl. Cut the chicory diagonally across into 1 cm (½ inch) slices and add to the bowl. Pour over the dressing and toss well.

Transfer to a salad bowl and sprinkle with the pine nuts to serve.
Serves 4 to 6

27

Lamb's Lettuce Salad

Lamb's lettuce or corn salad is a mild-flavoured salad plant which is easy to grow in the garden. The leaves are fragile and must be treated gently.

250 g (8 oz) lamb's
   lettuce, washed
1 head of radicchio
1 head of chicory
½ bulb of fennel
few dandelion leaves,
   halved (optional)
2 tablespoons
   chopped parsley
50 g (2 oz) walnuts
6 tablespoons French
   dressing*

Remove the roots from the lamb's lettuce and place the leaves in a salad bowl. Tear the radicchio into manageable pieces and slice the chicory diagonally into 1 cm (½ inch) pieces. Slice the fennel very thinly. Place these vegetables in the bowl with the remaining ingredients and toss thoroughly.
Serves 6 to 8
NOTE: Curly endive may be used in place of lamb's lettuce.

Alfalfa and Cress Salad

Alfalfa is one of the first cultivated plants. It is high in protein, vitamins and minerals.

125 g (4 oz) Chinese
   cabbage
125 g (4 oz) alfalfa
2 cartons salad cress
6 spring onions,
   sliced
6 tablespoons
   Vinaigrette
   dressing*

Slice the Chinese cabbage thinly and place in a salad bowl. Pull the alfalfa apart and add to the bowl with the cress and spring onions; mix well.
   Pour over the dressing and toss well just before serving.
Serves 4 to 6
NOTE: Bean sprouts could be used instead of alfalfa if preferred.

Endive and Gruyère Salad

1 head of curly endive
75 g (3 oz) Gruyère
   cheese, diced
25 g (1 oz) hazelnuts,
   chopped and
   browned
75 g (3 oz) smoked
   ham, diced
4 tablespoons French
   dressing*
1 tablespoon chopped
   parsley

Tear the endive into pieces and place in a bowl with the cheese, nuts and ham. Pour over the dressing and toss thoroughly. Transfer to a salad bowl and sprinkle with the parsley.
Serves 6 to 8

ROOT VEGETABLE SALADS

Root vegetables are ideal for use in autumn and winter salads. Apart from the ubiquitous potato, carrots, celeriac, fresh beetroot and Jerusalem artichokes are all suitable. To enable root vegetables to absorb the flavour of the dressing they should normally be cut into small pieces – diced, grated or cut into julienne. The latter are fine matchstick-sized pieces (illustrated on page 4).

Beetroot and Orange Salad

500 g (1 lb) raw
   beetroot, peeled
2 oranges
4 tablespoons Lemon
   vinaigrette
   dressing*
1 tablespoon chopped
   parsley

Grate the beetroot finely and place in a salad bowl. Finely grate the orange rind and mix with the dressing. Peel the pith from the oranges, break into segments and chop roughly; add to the beetroot.

Pour over the dressing and toss thoroughly. Sprinkle with the parsley to serve.
Serves 4 to 6

Carottes Râpées

This simple salad is delicious served as part of an hors d'oeuvre. It is also a suitable accompaniment for most cold meats. A little finely chopped shallot or onion may be added for extra flavour.

750 g (1½ lb) carrots
2 tablespoons chopped parsley
5 tablespoons French dressing*

Grate the carrots finely and place them in a bowl with the chopped parsley.

Pour over the dressing and toss thoroughly.

Transfer the salad to a serving dish and chill lightly before serving if preferred.

Serves 4 to 6

VARIATION:
Use young turnips, when they are in season, instead of carrots. Add 2 tablespoons Meaux mustard to the French dressing to make a piquant dressing, before adding to the salad.

Carrot, Turnip and Sesame Seed Salad

350 g (12 oz) carrots
175 g (6 oz) turnip
50 g (2 oz) seedless
  raisins
2 tablespoons sesame
  seeds, toasted
2 tablespoons snipped
  chives
4 tablespoons Honey
  and lemon
  dressing*

Grate the carrot and turnip finely and place in a salad bowl. Add the raisins, sesame seeds and chives and pour over the dressing. Toss well.
Serves 4 to 6

Jerusalem Artichoke Salad

This delicious salad makes an excellent accompaniment to cold meats. It also makes an unusual starter. Jerusalem artichokes are better scrubbed than peeled: they retain more flavour and food value.

500 g (1 lb)
    Jerusalem
    artichokes,
    scrubbed
salt and pepper
3 tablespoons olive
    oil
2 teaspoons lemon
    juice
1 tablespoon chopped
    parsley

Cut the artichokes into small even-sized pieces and place in a pan of salted water. Bring to the boil, cover and simmer for 12 to 15 minutes, until just tender. Drain and leave to cool in a mixing bowl.

Mix the remaining ingredients together, adding salt and pepper to taste, pour over the artichokes and toss well. Transfer to a serving dish.

Serves 4 to 6

VARIATION:
Add 2 tablespoons chopped walnuts to the salad before tossing.

Beetroot and Yogurt Salad

350 g (12 oz) cooked
    beetroot
2 dill cucumbers
2 tablespoons wine
    vinegar
4 tablespoons natural
    yogurt
salt and pepper
1 tablespoon chopped
    dill or fennel

Cut the beetroot and dill cucumbers
into 1 cm (½ inch) dice and place in a
mixing bowl.

Mix together the vinegar, yogurt,
and salt and pepper to taste. Pour
over the beetroot and cucumber and
mix thoroughly.

Turn into a shallow serving dish
and sprinkle with the dill or fennel
to serve.

Serves 4

VARIATION:

To turn this into a more substantial
salad add 500 g (1 lb) cooked and
diced potatoes. Increase the vinegar
to 3 tablespoons and the yogurt to
8 tablespoons.

Celeriac Rémoulade

This salad is popular throughout France and makes a wonderful addition to any picnic. Take care in this recipe to blanch the celeriac for exactly the right time so that it remains slightly crisp.

500 g (1 lb) celeriac, peeled
3 tablespoons Meaux mustard
3 tablespoons Mayonnaise*
2 tablespoons single cream
2 tablespoons natural yogurt
1 tablespoon chopped parsley

Cut the celeriac into julienne strips and blanch in boiling water for 2 minutes. Drain well and leave to cool.

Mix the mustard with the mayonnaise, cream and yogurt. Toss the celeriac in the mayonnaise mixture and spoon into a serving dish. Sprinkle with the parsley to serve.

Serves 4

NOTE: This salad also makes an unusual first course.

POTATO SALADS

The most nourishing part of the potato is just beneath the skin, so it is preferable just to scrub them and serve with the skins on, or scrape lightly if necessary. The flavour of the potato is also improved in this way.

A good addition to any potato salad is finely shredded dandelion, spinach or sorrel leaves. The sharpness of the green leaves contrasts well with the blandness of potatoes, especially when mixed with a creamy dressing.

The flavour of a potato salad is better if the dressing is added to the potatoes while they are still warm, as they can then absorb the dressing more easily.

Potato and Mustard Salad

500 g (1 lb) baby new potatoes
salt
2 tablespoons Meaux mustard
142 ml (5 fl oz) double cream

Cook the potatoes, in their skins, in boiling salted water until tender. Drain well and leave to cool in a mixing bowl. Halve the potatoes if necessary. Stir the mustard into the cream, pour over the potatoes and toss well. Transfer to a serving dish.
Serves 4

Warm Potato Salad

500 g (1 lb) new potatoes
salt
3 tablespoons French dressing*
3 tablespoons chopped mint

Cook the potatoes, in their skins, in boiling salted water until tender. Drain well and mix with the dressing and mint while warm. Transfer to a serving dish and serve immediately.
Serves 4

Potato Mayonnaise

750 g (1½ lb) new potatoes, scraped
salt
2 tablespoons French dressing*
1–2 tablespoons snipped chives
4 tablespoons Mayonnaise*
2 tablespoons natural yogurt

Cook the potatoes in boiling salted water until tender. Drain well, chop roughly and place in a mixing bowl. Add the dressing and most of the chives while still warm and toss well.

Transfer to a serving dish and leave to cool.

Mix the mayonnaise with the yogurt and spoon over the potatoes. Sprinkle with the remaining chives.
Serves 6

Potato and Sorrel Salad

A small quantity of sorrel makes an excellent addition to a rich salad and gives a pleasant piquant flavour. If you have no sorrel, use spinach or dandelion leaves instead.

500 g (1 lb) waxy
    potatoes
salt
2 tablespoons French
    dressing*
2 hard-boiled eggs
4 tomatoes, skinned
few sorrel leaves,
    finely shredded
3 tablespoons
    Mayonnaise*
3 tablespoons natural
    yogurt

Cook the potatoes in boiling salted water until tender. Drain well, chop roughly and place in a mixing bowl. Pour over the dressing while still warm and toss thoroughly. Leave to cool.

Cut each egg and each tomato into 8 wedges, discarding the tomato seeds. Add the eggs, tomatoes and sorrel to the potatoes and toss well. Transfer to a serving dish.

Mix together the mayonnaise and yogurt and spoon over the salad.
Serves 4

Curried Potato Salad

750 g (1½ lb) waxy
   potatoes, peeled
salt
6 tablespoons
   Mayonnaise*
1 teaspoon curry
   paste
1 tablespoon tomato
   ketchup
4 tablespoons natural
   yogurt
1 small onion, finely
   chopped
1 small green pepper,
   cored, seeded and
   chopped

Cook the potatoes in boiling salted
water until tender. Drain well, chop
roughly and leave to cool in a mixing
bowl.

   Mix together the mayonnaise,
curry paste, tomato ketchup and
yogurt, then pour over the potatoes.
Add the onion and green pepper and
toss well until coated. Transfer to a
serving dish.

Serves 6

OTHER VEGETABLE SALADS

Certain vegetables in this group benefit from blanching, as this enhances the flavour. It is always a personal choice, of course, but it is generally a good idea to blanch cauliflower, French beans and courgettes. Leeks and courgettes, alternatively, may be thinly sliced and marinated overnight in a dressing to soften them.

Fennel and Lemon Salad

2 bulbs of fennel
3 tablespoons chopped parsley
2 tablespoons lemon juice
2 tablespoons olive oil
salt and pepper

Trim the stalks, base and tough outer leaves from the fennel. Cut the bulbs in half, then shred very finely. Place in a salad bowl with the remaining ingredients, adding salt and pepper to taste, and toss thoroughly. Leave to marinate for 1 hour. Toss again before serving.

Serves 4

NOTE: This unusual salad is delicious served with fish dishes.

Celery, Apple and Watercress Salad

3 red-skinned dessert
  apples, quartered
  and cored
6 tablespoons Lemon
  vinaigrette
  dressing*
1 small head of
  celery, thinly sliced
1 bunch of watercress,
  divided into sprigs
25 g (1 oz) walnut
  pieces

Slice the apples into a small bowl, pour over the dressing and toss well. Add the celery, watercress and walnuts, mix well, then transfer to a salad bowl.

Serves 6 to 8

Mushroom and Bacon Salad

500 g (1 lb) button
  mushrooms
120 ml (4 fl oz)
  Garlic dressing*
125 g (4 oz) smoked
  streaky bacon,
  derinded and
  chopped
3 tablespoons
  chopped parsley

Trim the mushroom stalks level with the caps. Wipe the mushrooms with a damp cloth, place in a bowl with the dressing and toss well. Leave to stand for several hours, stirring occasionally, or overnight if possible.

Fry the bacon in its own fat until crisp. Add to the mushrooms with the parsley. Toss thoroughly and transfer to a serving dish.

Serves 4 to 6

Baby Tomatoes with Avocado Dressing

500 g (1 lb) baby
  tomatoes, skinned
150 ml (¼ pint)
  Avocado dressing*
1 tablespoon chopped
  parsley

Pile the tomatoes onto a shallow serving dish. Pour over the dressing and sprinkle with the parsley.

Serves 4

Cauliflower with Egg

1 small cauliflower,
  broken into florets
salt
3 hard-boiled eggs,
  chopped
150 ml (¼ pint)
  Roquefort
  dressing*
1 tablespoon chopped
  chives

Blanch the cauliflower in boiling salted water for 2 to 3 minutes; drain and leave to cool completely.

Place in a bowl, add the eggs and dressing and toss thoroughly. Transfer to a serving dish and sprinkle with the chives.

Serves 6

Mangetout Salad

250 g (8 oz)
  mangetout peas
1 red pepper, cored,
  seeded and finely
  sliced
1 tablespoon sesame
  seeds, toasted
4 tablespoons French
  dressing*

Top and tail the mangetout and, if large, cut in half diagonally. Place in a bowl with the remaining ingredients and toss thoroughly. Turn into a shallow serving dish.

Serves 4

Cauliflower, Avocado and Bean Sprout Salad

Bean sprouts are sprouted mung beans. They are most often used in Chinese stir-fried dishes, but they are delicious combined with other vegetables in salads. Bean sprouts are nutritionally highly valuable, because they are rich in vitamins B and C, and also contain plenty of protein.

250 g (8 oz)
    cauliflower,
    broken into tiny
    florets
salt
1 avocado pear,
    halved, stoned and
    peeled
6 tablespoons Herb
    dressing*
250 g (8 oz) fresh
    bean sprouts,
    trimmed

Cook the cauliflower in boiling salted water for 2 minutes; drain and leave to cool.

Slice the avocado into the dressing and toss thoroughly. Add the cauliflower and bean sprouts and toss until well coated. Transfer to a salad bowl.

Serves 4 to 6

Cauliflower and Mushroom Salad

250 g (8 oz)
  cauliflower,
  broken into florets
salt
125 g (4 oz) button
  mushrooms, sliced
1 large avocado pear,
  sliced
50 g (2 oz) split
  almonds, roasted
DRESSING:
4 tablespoons
  Mayonnaise*
4 tablespoons soured
  cream
1 teaspoon lemon
  juice
1 clove garlic, crushed
paprika
TO GARNISH:
1 tablespoon chopped
  chives

Cook the cauliflower in boiling salted water for 2 minutes; drain and leave to cool completely. Place in a bowl with the mushrooms, avocado and almonds.

Mix the dressing ingredients together, adding salt and paprika to taste. Pour over the vegetables and toss thoroughly. Transfer to a serving dish and sprinkle with the chives.
Serves 6 to 8

Mushroom Vinaigrette

250 g (8 oz) button
    mushrooms
4 spring onions,
    chopped
6 tablespoons
    Vinaigrette
    dressing*

Trim the mushroom stalks level with the caps. Wipe the mushrooms with a damp cloth, cut into thin slices and place in a salad bowl with the onion. Pour over the dressing and toss until well coated. Leave to stand for 30 minutes, stirring occasionally.
Serves 4

French Bean and Bacon Vinaigrette

250 g (8 oz) French
    beans, topped and
    tailed
salt
75 g (3 oz) streaky
    bacon, derinded
    and chopped
2 tablespoons
    Vinaigrette
    dressing*
few radicchio leaves

Place the beans in a pan of boiling salted water and simmer for 8 minutes. Drain and leave to cool.

Fry the bacon in its own fat until crisp. Place in a bowl with the beans, pour over the dressing and toss thoroughly.

Arrange the radicchio leaves on a serving dish and spoon the salad into the centre.
Serves 4
VARIATION: Replace the bacon with a 50 g (1¾ oz) can anchovies, drained, and each fillet cut into 3 pieces.

Onion and Watermelon Vinaigrette

This unusual and refreshing salad is delicious served as an accompaniment to rich meats.

1 kg (2 lb)
    watermelon, cut
    into wedges
1 tablespoon chopped
    mint
1 Spanish onion,
    thinly sliced
3 tablespoons Lemon
    vinaigrette*

Pick out the seeds from the watermelon and discard. Slice the watermelon wedges diagonally into strips. Place in a bowl and sprinkle with the mint.

Mix the onion and dressing together in another bowl and leave for 1 hour, stirring occasionally.

Mix the onion and dressing with the watermelon and transfer to a serving bowl.
Serves 4 to 6

Swedish Cucumber Salad

The flavour of dill blends beautifully with cucumber, though fennel could equally well be used if preferred. This salad is delicious served with salmon.

1 cucumber
salt
DRESSING:
1 tablespoon clear
  honey
1 tablespoon water
2 tablespoons
  chopped dill or
  fennel
4 tablespoons white
  wine vinegar

Slice the cucumber very thinly and place in a colander. Sprinkle liberally with salt and leave to drain for 30 minutes.

Meanwhile, mix the dressing ingredients together in a screw-topped jar. Shake well and leave for 30 minutes.

Dry the cucumber thoroughly on kitchen paper. Arrange the cucumber slices overlapping in a shallow dish and pour over the dressing.
Serves 4 to 6

Waldorf Salad

This famous American salad was created by the Maître d'Hotel of the Waldorf for its opening in 1893. It is a particularly good accompaniment to cold roast ham.

*150 ml (¼ pint)
   Mayonnaise**
*2 tablespoons natural
   yogurt*
*3 dessert apples,
   cored and roughly
   chopped*
*4 sticks of celery,
   chopped*
*25 g (1 oz) walnut
   pieces*
*1 tablespoon chopped
   parsley*

Mix the mayonnaise and yogurt together in a bowl. Add the apples, celery and walnuts and toss well to coat with mayonnaise.

Pile the salad onto a shallow serving dish and sprinkle with the parsley.

Serves 6 to 8

Algerian Salad

This salad originated in the Middle East. The unusual combination of sharp flavours goes particularly well with lamb dishes.

1 cucumber, diced
1 small green pepper,
cored, seeded and
diced
50 g (2 oz) green
olives, stoned and
chopped
1 tablespoon chopped
coriander
2 tablespoons
chopped mint
2 teaspoons wine
vinegar
2 tablespoons olive
oil
salt and pepper

Mix all the ingredients together thoroughly, seasoning with salt and pepper to taste. Transfer to a shallow serving dish.
Serves 6

Courgette and Tomato Salad

The very small, young courgettes are the most suitable to use raw in salads. They must be sliced very thinly to allow the flavour of the dressing to be absorbed.

250 g (8 oz) courgettes, thinly sliced
6 tablespoons Garlic dressing*
6 small tomatoes, sliced
50 g (2 oz) black olives, halved and stoned
1 tablespoon chopped marjoram
1 tablespoon chopped parsley

Place the courgettes in a bowl, pour over the dressing and leave to marinate overnight.

Add the remaining ingredients, toss thoroughly and turn into a salad bowl.

Serves 4 to 6

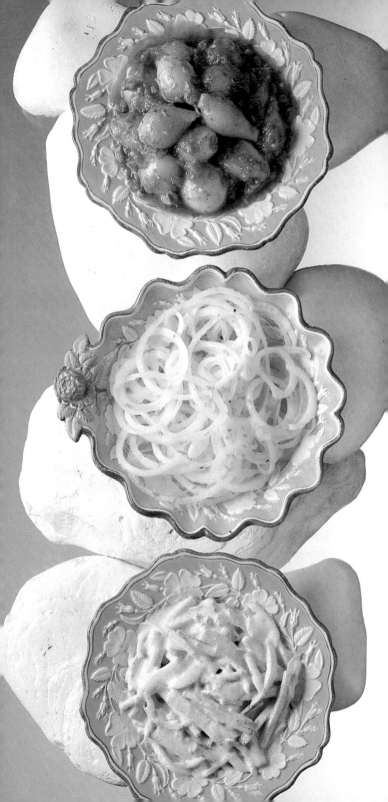

Baby Onions with Capers

The piquant flavour of this salad goes especially well with cold meats and cheeses.

500 g (1 lb) pickling onions
3 tomatoes, skinned and chopped
1 tablespoon capers
2 teaspoons tomato purée
1/2 teaspoon soft brown sugar
2 teaspoons wine vinegar
2 tablespoons olive oil
2 tablespoons chopped parsley

Plunge the onions into boiling water and boil for 1 to 2 minutes. Drain, cool slightly, then remove the skins.

Return to the pan with the tomatoes, capers, tomato purée, sugar, vinegar and oil. Cover and simmer for 5 minutes, then stir in the parsley. Transfer to a serving dish and chill before serving.

Serves 4

Onion and Chilli Salad

A hot onion side dish which makes a tasty accompaniment to a curry or cold meats.

5 tablespoons cider vinegar
3 tablespoons water
1 green chilli, seeded and chopped
salt and pepper
2 Spanish onions, thinly sliced

Mix together the vinegar, water, chilli, and salt and pepper to taste.

Place the onions in a shallow serving dish and pour over the dressing. Leave to stand for 1 hour, stirring occasionally.

Serves 6

Celery Julienne

4 celery sticks
1/2 cucumber
salt
1/2 bulb of fennel
6 tablespoons Herb dressing*

Cut the celery and cucumber into julienne strips 3.5 cm (1½ inches) long. Place the cucumber in a colander, sprinkle with salt and leave to drain for 30 minutes.

Trim the stalks, base and tough outer leaves from the fennel. Cut in half then shred finely.

Dry the cucumber on kitchen paper and place in a bowl with the fennel and celery. Pour over the dressing and toss well. Transfer to a serving dish.

Serves 4

Tomato and Basil Salad

The piquant flavour of basil greatly enhances the flavour of the tomatoes, and the mellowness of the olive oil brings out the full flavour of this delicious salad. Serve as a tasty main course accompaniment or a refreshing summer first course.

500 g (1 lb)
    Marmande
    tomatoes
salt and pepper
3 tablespoons olive
    oil
2 tablespoons
    chopped basil

Slice the tomatoes thinly and lay them in a shallow serving dish, sprinkling each layer with salt and pepper. Pour over the oil and sprinkle with the basil.

Serves 4

NOTE: Marmande tomatoes are the large round variety, often called Mediterranean tomatoes.

Cucumber with Mint

The refreshing quality of this salad makes it especially suitable to serve with curries. It is also very pleasant served on its own after a fish course.

1 cucumber, thinly
    sliced
salt
1 bunch of mint,
    finely chopped
8 tablespoons Yogurt
    dressing*

Place the cucumber in a colander, sprinkle with salt and leave to drain for 30 minutes. Dry the cucumber on kitchen paper and place in a shallow serving dish. Add the mint and dressing and mix well.

Serves 4 to 6

VARIATION:
1. Trim 4 spring onions, slice them finely and mix with the cucumber.
2. Thinly slice 4 tomatoes and layer them in the serving dish with the cucumber slices.

Tomato and Leek Salad

500 g (1 lb) tomatoes,
    sliced
125 g (4 oz) leeks,
    thinly sliced
4 tablespoons Honey
    and lemon
    dressing*
1 tablespoon chopped
    parsley

Arrange the tomatoes and leeks in layers in a shallow serving dish, finishing with leeks. Pour over the dressing evenly and sprinkle with the parsley.

Serves 4

NOTE: The leeks may be marinated in the dressing for 15 minutes before combining with the tomatoes if a more mellow flavour is preferred.

FISH, MEAT & CHEESE SALADS

The salads in this chapter make delicious light main dishes, especially suitable for hot summer days. Many of them can be packed into rigid polythene containers and taken on picnics. Most of these nutritious salads can be served as starters; the quantities should be adjusted accordingly.

Prawn and Tomato Salad

½ cucumber
4 tomatoes, skinned,
  seeded and
  shredded
350 g (12 oz) peeled
  prawns
150 ml (¼ pint)
  Tomato
  mayonnaise*
few lettuce leaves
few cooked whole
  prawns to garnish

Cut the cucumber into julienne strips 2.5 cm (1 inch) long. Place in a bowl with the tomatoes and prawns. Pour over the mayonnaise and toss well to coat.

Arrange the lettuce on a serving dish, spoon the salad into the centre and garnish with whole prawns.
Serves 4

Crab and Avocado Salad

350 g (12 oz) crab
  claw meat, or
  2 × 177 g (6 oz)
  cans crabmeat
150 ml (¼ pint)
  Avocado dressing*
2 avocado pears,
  halved, stoned and
  peeled
2 tablespoons French
  dressing*
1 tablespoon
  pumpkin seeds
  (optional)

Cut the crab meat into pieces, or drain the canned crabmeat and break into pieces. Place in a bowl, pour over half the avocado dressing and mix well.

Slice the avocados lengthways and arrange cut side down on a serving dish, pressing lightly to separate the slices out to the edge of the dish. Brush with the French dressing.

Spoon the crab into the centre, coat with the remaining avocado dressing and sprinkle with the pumpkin seeds, if using.

Serves 4

Sardine and Tomato Salad

1 lettuce
500 g (1 lb) tomatoes, sliced
½ Spanish onion, cut into rings
2 × 120 g (4¼ oz) cans sardines in oil, drained
4 tablespoons French dressing*
1 tablespoon chopped parsley

Arrange the lettuce on a shallow serving dish and cover with the tomato slices and onion rings. Arrange the sardines in a circle, with tails towards the centre. Spoon over the dressing to cover and sprinkle with the parsley.

Serve with crusty bread.

Serves 4

VARIATION:
Add 2 tablespoons tomato ketchup and 1 tablespoon well drained capers to the French dressing.

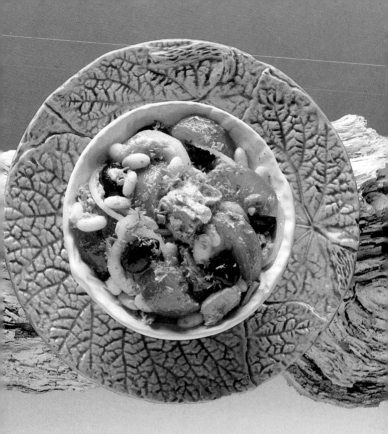

Tuna and Bean Salad

250 g (8 oz) haricot
  beans, soaked
  overnight
salt
6 tomatoes, skinned
50 g (2 oz) black
  olives, halved and
  stoned
1 onion, thinly sliced
2 tablespoons
  chopped parsley
1 × 198 g (7 oz) can
  tuna fish, drained
4 tablespoons Garlic
  dressing*

Drain the beans, place in a pan and cover with cold water. Bring to the boil, cover and simmer for 1 to 1½ hours, until tender, adding a little salt towards the end of cooking. Drain well and leave to cool.

Cut each tomato into 8 pieces and place in a bowl with the beans, olives, onion and parsley.

Flake the tuna into large pieces and add to the salad. Pour over the dressing and toss well.

Transfer to a serving dish and serve with a green salad and crusty bread.
Serves 6

Salmon and Dill Salad

2 tablespoons fine sea
  salt
2 tablespoons caster
  sugar
1 teaspoon ground
  black pepper
2 tablespoons
  chopped dill
750 g (1½ lb) tail
  piece of salmon,
  filleted
1 bulb of fennel
2 tablespoons Lemon
  vinaigrette
  dressing*
DILL DRESSING:
2 tablespoons
  German mustard
1 tablespoon caster
  sugar
1 tablespoon wine
  vinegar
6 tablespoons olive
  oil
2 tablespoons soured
  cream
2 tablespoons
  chopped dill

Mix together the salt, sugar, pepper and dill and sprinkle half of the mixture over the base of a shallow dish. Lay the salmon on top and sprinkle with the remaining dill mixture. Cover and leave to marinate for 2 to 3 days in the refrigerator, turning the salmon each day.

Trim the stalks, base and coarse outer leaves from the fennel; reserve a few feathery leaves for garnish. Cut the bulb in half lengthways, then slice very thinly into strips. Place in a bowl and pour over the vinaigrette. Toss well and leave to marinate for 1 hour.

To make the dill dressing, beat the mustard, sugar and vinegar together. Gradually add the oil, beating well between each addition. Gradually beat in the cream, then stir in the dill.

Remove the skin from the salmon. Cut the fish into 3 mm (⅛ inch) wide strips, across the grain. Arrange on a serving dish. Pour over the dill dressing and arrange the fennel strips around the edge. Garnish with the fennel leaves. Serve with rye bread.
Serves 4

Swedish Herring Salad

4 rollmops
125 g (4 oz) cooked
  beetroot, diced
250 g (8 oz) cooked
  potato, diced
1 small onion,
  chopped
2 dill cucumbers,
  chopped
150 ml (¼ pint)
  Soured cream
  dressing*
2 hard-boiled eggs
1 tablespoon chopped
  dill or fennel

Unroll the rollmops, cut in half lengthways, then cut into thin strips. Place in a bowl with the beetroot, potato, onion and dill cucumber and mix well. Pour over the dressing and toss thoroughly.

Transfer the salad to a shallow serving dish. Chop the eggs and sprinkle over the salad. Garnish with the dill or fennel.
Serves 4

Salade Niçoise

625 g (1¼ lb)
  tomatoes, sliced
3 hard-boiled eggs,
  sliced
1 × 198 g (7 oz) can
  tuna fish, drained
  and flaked
250 g (8 oz) French
  beans, cooked
2 tablespoons
  chopped mixed
  herbs (parsley,
  chives, marjoram)
6 tablespoons French
  dressing*
½ cucumber, sliced
1 × 50 g (1¾ oz) can
  anchovy fillets,
  drained
8 black olives, halved
  and stoned

Arrange half the tomatoes in a layer
in a shallow serving dish and cover
with the eggs, tuna fish, beans and
herbs. Pour over half the dressing.
Cover with the cucumber slices, then
the remaining tomatoes.

Split the anchovies in half
lengthways and arrange in a lattice
pattern over the tomatoes. Place an
olive half in each diamond and spoon
over the remaining dressing.

Serve with crusty brown bread.

Serves 4

VARIATION: To serve as an informal
country salad, cut the tomatoes and
eggs into quarters and mix with the
other ingredients. Serve in a lettuce-
lined salad bowl.

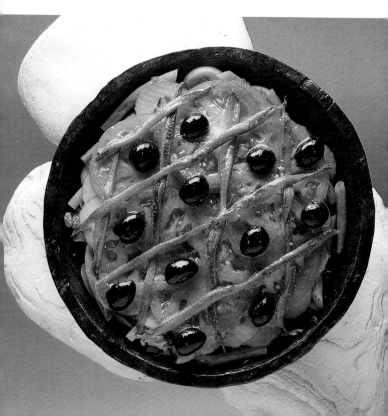

Chicken and Avocado Salad

2 avocado pears,
    halved, stoned and
    peeled
2–3 teaspoons lemon
    juice
250 g (8 oz) cooked
    chicken, cut into
    pieces
1 × 230 g (7½ oz)
    can water
    chestnuts, drained
    and sliced
6 tablespoons natural
    yogurt
½ teaspoon
    Worcestershire
    sauce
salt and pepper
6 tablespoons
    Mayonnaise*

Slice one of the avocado pears.
Reserve 3 slices and brush with some
of the lemon juice.

Place the remaining sliced avocado
in a bowl, pour over the remaining
lemon juice and toss well; this will
prevent the avocado discolouring.
Add the chicken and water chestnuts
and mix together.

Place the remaining avocado
halves in an electric blender or food
processor with the yogurt,
Worcestershire sauce, and salt and
pepper to taste. Blend until smooth,
then add to the mayonnaise and mix
thoroughly.

Pour the dressing over the chicken
mixture and toss well to combine.
Spoon onto a shallow serving dish
and garnish with the reserved
avocado slices.
Serves 4

Chicken Liver and Spinach Salad

250g (8 oz) spinach
3 tablespoons French dressing*
1 × 125g (4 oz) bacon steak
2 tablespoons olive oil
4 chicken livers, cut into strips
2 tablespoons cider vinegar
pepper

Trim the stalks from the spinach. Wash and dry the leaves thoroughly, then cut into strips. Place in a salad bowl, pour over the dressing, toss well and leave for 10 minutes.

Cut the bacon steak into 5 mm (¼ inch) wide strips. Heat 1 tablespoon of the oil in a pan, add the bacon and fry until golden. Place on top of the spinach.

Heat the remaining oil in the pan, add the chicken livers and fry for 3 to 4 minutes, until well browned. Add to the salad bowl.

Add the vinegar to the pan and stir to dissolve any juices. Pour over the salad, season well with pepper and toss thoroughly.

Serve with crusty bread for a light lunch.

Serves 4

NOTE: This salad can alternatively be served as an unusual starter (for 6).

Curried Chicken Salad

3 celery sticks
350g (12 oz) cooked chicken, cut into strips
1 × 227g (8 oz) can pineapple, drained
50g (2 oz) split almonds, browned
6 tablespoons Mayonnaise*
4 tablespoons natural yogurt
1 teaspoon curry paste
1 tablespoon tomato ketchup
few lettuce leaves

Cut the celery into 3.5 cm × 5 mm (1½ × ¼ inch) julienne strips. Place in a bowl with the chicken, pineapple and almonds. Toss the ingredients together.

Mix the mayonnaise, yogurt, curry paste and tomato ketchup together, pour over the chicken salad and mix thoroughly.

Place the lettuce on a serving dish and spoon the chicken mixture into the centre.

Serves 4 to 6

Cottage Cheese Salad

340 g (12 oz) cottage
  cheese
3 tomatoes, skinned,
  seeded and chopped
¼ cucumber, chopped
salt and pepper
few curly endive
  leaves

Place the cheese, tomatoes and
cucumber in a bowl and mix well,
seasoning with salt and pepper to
taste.
   Arrange the endive leaves on
4 individual serving dishes and
spoon the salad into the centre.
Serve with crusty brown bread.
Serves 4

Greek Salad

6 tomatoes, cut into
  wedges
½ cucumber, diced
1 small onion, sliced
1 small green pepper,
  cored, seeded and
  roughly chopped
3 tablespoons olive
  oil
1 tablespoon wine
  vinegar
salt and pepper
175 g (6 oz) feta
  cheese, cut into
  cubes
125 g (4 oz) black
  olives
1 teaspoon dried
  oregano

Place the tomatoes, cucumber, onion
and green pepper in a bowl and mix
well. Pour over the oil, vinegar, and
salt and pepper to taste, and toss
thoroughly.
   Transfer the salad to a bowl and
cover with the cheese and olives.
Sprinkle with the oregano to serve.
Serves 4

Tomato and Mozzarella Salad

500 g (1 lb)
  Marmande
  tomatoes, thinly
  sliced
salt and pepper
250 g (8 oz)
  Mozzarella
  cheese, sliced
3 tablespoons olive
  oil
4 tablespoons
  chopped parsley

Layer the tomatoes in a shallow
serving dish, sprinkling each layer
with salt and pepper. Arrange the
Mozzarella in overlapping layers on
top of the tomatoes. Pour over the oil
and sprinkle with the parsley.
   Serve with a green salad, salami if
liked, and granary bread.
Serves 4
NOTE: Marmande tomatoes are the
large round variety, often called
Mediterranean tomatoes.

PULSE & RICE SALADS

All pulse vegetables, except lentils and split peas, should be soaked overnight before cooking. Always discard the soaking water and cook pulses in fresh clean water. Add salt towards the end of the cooking, rather than at the beginning, to avoid toughening the skins.

Mixed Bean Salad

125 g (4 oz) red
    kidney beans,
    soaked overnight
125 g (4 oz) haricot
    beans, soaked
    overnight
salt
125 g (4 oz) French
    beans
125 g (4 oz) shelled
    broad beans
6 tablespoons Garlic
    dressing*
2 tablespoons
    chopped parsley

Drain the kidney beans and haricot beans. Place in separate pans, cover with cold water, bring to the boil and simmer for 1 to 1½ hours, until tender, adding a little salt towards the end of cooking. Drain and place in a bowl.

Cut the French beans into 2.5 cm (1 inch) lengths. Cook the broad beans and French beans in boiling salted water for 7 to 8 minutes, until just tender. Drain and add to the bowl. Pour over the dressing while still warm and mix well. Cool, then stir in the parsley. Transfer to a serving dish.
Serves 8

Kidney Bean and Chilli Salad

175 g (6 oz) red
  kidney beans,
  soaked overnight
salt
6 tablespoons Chilli
  dressing*
125 g (4 oz) frozen
  sweetcorn, cooked,
  or 1 × 198 g
  (7 oz) can, drained
1 red pepper, cored,
  seeded and chopped
2 tablespoons
  chopped parsley

Drain the kidney beans, place in a pan and cover with cold water. Bring to the boil, cover and simmer for 1 to 1½ hours, until tender, adding a little salt towards the end of cooking.

Drain the beans thoroughly and place in a bowl. Pour over the dressing and mix well while still warm. Leave to cool.

Add the sweetcorn and red pepper. Toss thoroughly and adjust the seasoning if necessary. Transfer to a serving dish and sprinkle with the chopped parsley to serve.

Serves 4 to 6

Black Bean and Bacon Salad

175 g (6 oz) black
  beans, soaked
  overnight
salt
6 tablespoons Garlic
  dressing*
75 g (3 oz) thick-cut
  streaky bacon, cut
  into strips
1 red pepper, cored,
  seeded and sliced
3 celery sticks, sliced

Drain the beans, place in a pan and cover with cold water. Bring to the boil, cover and simmer for 1½ to 2 hours, until tender, adding a little salt towards the end of cooking.

Drain the beans thoroughly and place in a bowl. Pour over the dressing and toss while still warm.

Fry the bacon in its own fat until crisp. Stir into the beans and leave to cool.

Stir in the red pepper and celery and transfer to a salad bowl.
Serves 6 to 8

Chick Pea Salad

250 g (8 oz) chick
  peas, soaked
  overnight
salt
4 tablespoons Ginger
  dressing*
1 small onion, finely
  chopped
1 red pepper, cored,
  seeded and diced
2 tablespoons
  chopped parsley

Drain the chick peas, place in a pan and cover with cold water. Bring to the boil and simmer for 1½ to 2 hours or until softened, adding a little salt towards the end of cooking.

Drain thoroughly and place in a bowl. Pour over the dressing and toss well while still warm. Leave to cool.

Add the remaining ingredients, toss thoroughly and transfer to a serving dish.
Serves 6

Black Eye Bean and Mushroom Salad

175 g (6 oz) black
  eye beans, soaked
  overnight
salt
125 g (4 oz) button
  mushrooms, sliced
4 tablespoons French
  dressing*
1 small red pepper,
  cored, seeded and
  sliced
2 tablespoons
  chopped parsley

Drain the beans, place in a pan and cover with cold water. Bring to the boil, cover and simmer for 40 to 45 minutes until tender, adding a little salt towards the end of cooking.

Drain thoroughly and place in a bowl with the mushrooms. Pour over the dressing and toss well while still warm. Leave to cool.

Add the red pepper and parsley, toss thoroughly and transfer to a salad bowl.
Serves 6

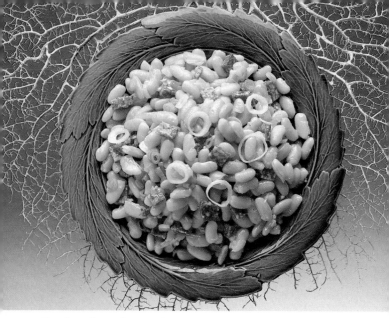

Salade de Flageolets

250 g (8 oz) flageolet
  beans, soaked
  overnight
salt
6 tablespoons Garlic
  dressing*
50 g (2 oz) salami,
  cut into 5 mm
  (¼ inch) squares
4 spring onions,
  sliced

Drain the beans, place in a pan and
cover with cold water. Bring to the
boil, cover and simmer for 1¼ to 1½
hours, until tender, adding a little salt
towards the end of cooking. Drain
thoroughly and place in a bowl. Pour
over the dressing and mix well while
still warm. Leave to cool.

Add the salami and spring onions
to the beans. Toss well to serve.
Serves 4 to 6

Lentil Salad

250 g (8 oz) green
  lentils
salt and pepper
6 tablespoons Soy
  sauce dressing*
4 tomatoes, skinned
  and chopped
1 small onion,
  chopped
125 g (4 oz) bean
  sprouts
2 celery sticks, sliced
1 tablespoon chopped
  summer savory

Cover the lentils with boiling water
and leave to soak for 20 minutes.
Drain, place in a pan and cover with
cold water. Bring to the boil, add a
little salt, then cover and simmer for
20 minutes, until softened. Drain well
and place in a bowl. Pour over the
dressing and mix well while still
warm. Leave to cool.

Add the remaining ingredients,
seasoning with salt and pepper to
taste, toss thoroughly and transfer to
a serving dish.
Serves 6 to 8

Tabbouleh

Bulgur or Burghul wheat is parboiled wheat. It is eaten widely in Eastern Europe. Tabbouleh originated in the Middle East.

125 g (4 oz) bulgur
  wheat
50 g (2 oz) parsley
4 tablespoons
  chopped mint
1 onion, finely
  chopped
3 tablespoons lemon
  juice
4 tablespoons olive
  oil
3 tomatoes, skinned,
  seeded and chopped
salt and pepper

Soak the wheat in cold water for 1 hour. Drain thoroughly, then place in a mixing bowl.

Chop the parsley finely and add to the wheat, together with the remaining ingredients. Season with salt and pepper to taste. Mix well to combine the ingredients and transfer to a serving dish.

Serves 6

Brown Rice Salad

175 g (6 oz) brown rice
salt
6 spring onions
1 red pepper, cored, seeded and diced
50 g (2 oz) currants
50 g (2 oz) roasted cashew nuts
2 tablespoons roasted sunflower seeds
6 tablespoons Soy sauce dressing*
3 tablespoons chopped parsley

Cook the rice in boiling salted water for 30 to 40 minutes, until tender. Rinse and drain well. Chop the spring onions finely.

Transfer the rice to a bowl while still warm and add the spring onions and remaining ingredients. Toss thoroughly and transfer to a serving dish.

Serves 6 to 8

NOTE: Sweetcorn and diced green pepper may be added to this salad.

74

Spiced Rice Salad

75 g (3 oz) dried
    apricots, chopped
125 g (4 oz) long-
    grain rice
salt
1 tablespoon corn oil
50 g (2 oz) split
    almonds
1 teaspoon grated
    nutmeg
3 celery sticks, diced
4 spring onions,
    sliced
1 tablespoon chopped
    coriander
4 tablespoons French
    dressing*

Cover the apricots with boiling water, leave to soak for 1 hour, then drain well.

Place the rice in a pan of boiling salted water and simmer for 12 to 15 minutes, until tender. Rinse thoroughly, drain and leave to cool slightly.

Heat the oil in a small pan, add the almonds and fry until pale golden. Add the nutmeg and fry for a few seconds.

Place the warm rice in a salad bowl with the apricots. Add the spiced almonds with their oil. Mix in the celery, spring onions and coriander. Pour the dressing over the salad and toss thoroughly before serving.

Serves 4

VARIATION: Use stoned and chopped dates instead of the dried apricots; these will not require pre-soaking.

Green Rice Salad

This attractive, slightly different salad makes a good accompaniment to cold fish dishes, such as salmon.

175 g (6 oz) long-
    grain rice
salt
1/2 cucumber, diced
4 celery sticks, diced
1 green pepper,
    cored, seeded and
    diced
6 spring onions,
    sliced
2 tablespoons
    chopped mint
6 tablespoons
    Vinaigrette
    dressing*

Place the rice in a pan of boiling salted water and simmer for 12 to 15 minutes, until tender. Rinse thoroughly and drain well.

Place the rice in a bowl while still warm and add the remaining ingredients. Toss thoroughly and transfer to a serving dish.

Serves 6 to 8

SALAD DRESSINGS

A well made salad dressing can transform a good salad into something really exciting. But it is most important to use good ingredients; the choice of oil is especially important. Oils are produced from various nuts, seeds and beans, and each has its own particular flavour. Unrefined oils have a superior flavour and although more expensive than refined oils, they are worth using for salad dressings.

Olive oil is generally agreed to be far superior to other oils for dressings as it has such a fine flavour. The best is virgin oil, made from crushed olives. It has a green tinge and rich flavour and smell. It is rather heavy for mayonnaise, however, and some people feel it is too strong, so it can be mixed with sunflower oil, which has a mild nutty flavour and is good for all dressings.

Sesame oil is a lovely amber colour and has a fairly strong nutty tang. It gives an unusual flavour to dressings and is even more delicious if a few roasted sesame seeds are added.

Always choose wine, cider or herb-flavoured vinegars – malt vinegar is far too harsh; lemon juice can be used instead if preferred. Herb-flavoured vinegars are especially useful in winter when fresh herbs are not available. It is a common fault to use too much vinegar in a dressing. The proportion should be one part vinegar and 3 to 4 parts oil. If it tastes too oily, add a little more salt.

Always use freshly ground black pepper and whole seed mustard, such as Moutarde de Meaux or Dijon, which give the dressing a deliciously rich flavour.

French dressing can be stored in a bottle for several weeks so it is worth making up a large quantity at a time. Yogurt, cream or egg-based dressings can be stored for several days in a sealed container in the refrigerator.

Salad dressings should be poured over green salads at the last minute to prevent the leaves wilting. In some salads, however, the flavour of the dressing needs to be absorbed by the ingredients, so they can be dressed in advance and marinated for a few hours or sometimes overnight.

Vinaigrette Dressing

175 ml (6 fl oz) olive
  oil
4 tablespoons cider
  vinegar
1 teaspoon clear
  honey
1 clove garlic, crushed
2 tablespoons
  chopped mixed
  herbs (mint,
  parsley, chives,
  thyme)
salt and pepper

Put all the ingredients in a screw-topped jar, adding salt and pepper to taste. Shake well to blend before using.
Makes 250 ml (8 fl oz)

Lemon or Lime Vinaigrette: Use 4 tablespoons fresh lemon or lime juice in place of the cider vinegar.

French Dressing

175 ml (6 fl oz) olive oil
4 tablespoons wine vinegar
1 teaspoon French mustard
1 clove garlic, crushed
1 teaspoon clear honey
salt and pepper

Put all the ingredients in a screw-topped jar, adding salt and pepper to taste. Shake well to blend before serving.
Makes 250 ml (8 fl oz)

Mustard Dressing: Add 2 tablespoons Meaux mustard.
Garlic Dressing: Crush 4 cloves garlic and add to the ingredients.

Honey and Lemon Dressing

4 tablespoons lemon juice
2 tablespoons clear honey
3 tablespoons olive oil
salt and pepper

Put all the ingredients in a screw-topped jar, adding salt and pepper to taste. Shake well to blend before serving.
Makes 150 ml (¼ pint)

Roquefort Dressing

50 g (2 oz) Roquefort
    cheese
142 ml (5 fl oz)
    single cream
1 tablespoon chopped
    chives
salt and pepper

Mash the cheese with a fork and
gradually add the cream to form a
smooth paste. Mix in the chives, and
salt and pepper to taste. Store in an
airtight container in the refrigerator.
Makes 250 ml (8 fl oz)

Soy Sauce Dressing

175 ml (6 fl oz)
    sunflower oil
4 tablespoons soy
    sauce
2 tablespoons lemon
    juice
1 clove garlic, crushed
salt and pepper

Put all the ingredients in a screw-
topped jar, adding salt and pepper to
taste. Shake well to blend.
Makes 300 ml (½ pint)

Ginger Dressing: Add a 2.5 cm (1
inch) piece peeled and finely chopped
root ginger to the ingredients.
Chilli Dressing: Add 1 seeded and
finely chopped green chilli.

Soured Cream Dressing

142 ml (5 fl oz)
  soured cream
1 tablespoon lemon
  juice
1 clove garlic, crushed
1 teaspoon clear
  honey
salt and pepper
little milk (optional)

Place all the ingredients in a bowl, adding salt and pepper to taste, and mix thoroughly with a fork. Add milk to thin if necessary.
Makes 150 ml (¼ pint)

Avocado Dressing: Place 1 peeled and chopped avocado pear, 5 table-spoons single cream and 1 teaspoon Worcestershire sauce in an electric blender or food processor. Blend until smooth, then mix with the soured cream dressing.
Makes 350 ml (12 fl oz)

Quick Mayonnaise

1 egg
½ teaspoon salt
½ teaspoon pepper
½ teaspoon mustard
  powder
2 teaspoons wine
  vinegar
150 ml (¼ pint)
  olive oil
150 ml (¼ pint)
  sunflower oil

Place the egg, seasonings and vinegar in an electric blender or food processor and blend on medium speed for a few seconds. Still on medium speed, add the oils drop by drop to begin with, through the lid, then in a thin stream as the mixture thickens.

Store in an airtight container in the refrigerator for up to 10 days.
Makes about 300 ml (½ pint)

Tomato Mayonnaise: Skin, seed and chop 2 tomatoes and place in the blender with 1 crushed clove garlic, ½ teaspoon brown sugar and 2 teaspoons tomato purée. Blend on maximum speed for 30 seconds, then stir into half the mayonnaise.
Makes about 250 ml (8 fl oz)

Traditional Method Mayonnaise: Replace the 1 egg with 2 egg yolks. Beat the egg yolks and seasonings together in a bowl. Add the oils drop by drop, beating constantly. As the mixture thickens, add the oils in a steady stream. Add the vinegar and mix thoroughly.

Yogurt Dressing

150 g (5.2 oz)
   natural yogurt
1 clove garlic, crushed
1 tablespoon cider
   vinegar
1 teaspoon clear
   honey
salt and pepper

Place all the ingredients in a bowl, adding salt and pepper to taste, and mix thoroughly with a fork.
Makes about 150 ml (¼ pint)

Herb Dressing: Place the above ingredients in an electric blender or food processor with 15 g (½ oz) parsley and 15 g (½ oz) mixed mint and chives. Blend on maximum speed for 1 to 2 minutes. Chill until required. Shake well before using.
Makes 250 ml (8 fl oz)

FRUIT SALADS

A fruit salad should be fresh, light and attractively appetizing in appearance. Use best quality fruits, preferably freshly picked.

Some fruits have a particular affinity with each other. For example, the flavour of strawberries and blackcurrants is enhanced by orange; pawpaw tastes quite exotic mixed with lime. Rose water and orange flower water impart a subtle scented flavour to most fruits. Liqueurs improve the flavour of fruits enormously, especially those with a fruity base such as Cointreau and Grand Marnier. If you are lucky enough to have a bottle of Framboise this blends well with any red fruit.

Do not cut up the fruit into small identical cubes; maintain the shape of the segment to give a more attractive and appetizing appearance.

Although summer is naturally the best time for fruit salads, some excellent fruit salads can be created in winter. With dried fruits and so many canned tropical fruits available, together with whatever is in the shops, it should be possible to make a tempting fruit salad at any time of year.

Red Fruit Salad

4 tablespoons clear
 honey
150 ml (¼ pint) red
 wine
150 ml (¼ pint)
 orange juice
250 g (8 oz)
 blackcurrants
250 g (8 oz)
 strawberries
250 g (8 oz)
 raspberries
1 tablespoon
 arrowroot

Place the honey, wine and orange juice in a pan. Add the blackcurrants, bring to the boil, cover and simmer for 10 minutes, until soft.

Strain the fruit, reserving the syrup. Place the blackcurrants in a glass bowl and add the remaining fruit.

Return the syrup to the pan and bring to the boil. Blend the arrowroot with a little cold water and stir into the boiling syrup. Cook, stirring, until the syrup is clear. Pour over the fruit, leave to cool then chill.

Serve with whipped cream.
Serves 8

Green Fruit Salad

150 ml (¼ pint)
  apple juice
1 tablespoon clear
  honey
3 tablespoons kirsch
  or Chartreuse
1 green dessert apple,
  quartered and cored
1 pear, quartered and
  cored
1 Honeydew melon,
  halved and seeded
125 g (4 oz) seedless
  grapes
2 kiwi fruit, peeled
  and sliced
few lemon balm
  leaves, chopped

Mix the apple juice, honey and kirsch or Chartreuse together in a bowl. Slice the apple and pear thinly into the juice and stir to coat completely. Cut the melon flesh into cubes, add to the bowl with the grapes and kiwi fruit and leave for 1 hour, stirring occasionally.

Turn into a serving dish and sprinkle with the lemon balm to serve.
Serves 4 to 6

Peach and Passion Fruit Chantilly

3 passion fruit
6 peaches, skinned,
 halved and stoned
120 ml (4 fl oz)
 double cream
2 tablespoons orange
 flower water
 (optional)

Cut the passion fruit in half using a sharp knife, and scoop out the flesh into a bowl. Slice the peaches thinly and add to the bowl. Carefully toss the fruit together and spoon into 4 individual glasses or serving dishes.

Whip the cream together with the orange flower water if using, until it stands in peaks. Spoon a little cream onto each fruit salad before serving.

Serves 4

NOTE: Passion fruit are ready to eat when their skins are dimpled. The whole flesh, including the pips, may be eaten.

Polynesian Pawpaw Salad

Pawpaw is also known as papaya. It has a delicious pinkish orange flesh enclosed in a yellow and green freckled skin. Apart from being perfect in fruit salad, they are delicious simply sprinkled with lime juice.

1 pawpaw
juice of ½ lime
1 pink-fleshed
  grapefruit
lime slices to decorate

Cut the pawpaw into quarters and remove the seeds. Peel and slice into a glass bowl. Pour over the lime juice.

Peel the grapefruit, removing all pith, and cut into segments. Add to the bowl and chill until required.

Decorate with lime slices to serve.

Serves 4

NOTE: Pawpaw are ready to eat when they yield to gentle pressure applied in the palm of your hand.

Caribbean Salad

1 Charentais or
  Gallia melon,
  halved and seeded
1 mango, peeled
1 banana
3 tablespoons white
  rum
lemon balm sprigs to
  decorate (optional)

Cut the flesh out of the melon halves and cut into slices. Reserve the shells.

Cut the mango in half lengthways, as close to the stone as possible. Using a sharp knife, remove the stone. Cut the flesh into slices and place in a bowl with the melon.

Slice the banana and add to the fruit with the rum. Stir well, then spoon into the reserved melon shells and decorate with lemon balm if using.

Serves 4 to 6

NOTE: Mangos are ripe when they yield to gentle pressure applied in the palm of your hand.

Guava Passion

2 oranges
1 × 411 g (14½ oz)
  can guavas
2 bananas (optional)
125 g (4 oz) black
  grapes, halved and
  seeded
2 passion fruit

Peel the oranges, removing all pith, and cut into segments.

Place the oranges in a serving bowl with the juice from the guavas. Slice the guavas and bananas if using, and add to the bowl with the grapes.

Halve the passion fruit, scoop out the flesh and mix with the other fruit. Serve with whipped cream.

Serves 6

Fraises Plougastel

This tempting summer dessert is named after the little town of Plougastel in Brittany, which is famous for its excellent strawberries.

500 g (1 lb)
strawberries
2 tablespoons caster
sugar
grated rind and juice
of ½ orange
2 tablespoons Grand
Marnier

Divide half the strawberries between 4 individual serving dishes.

Place the remaining strawberries in a bowl with the sugar and orange rind, then mash to a pulp using a fork. Add the orange juice and liqueur and mix thoroughly. Pour this pulped mixture over the whole strawberries. Chill in the refrigerator until required.

Serve with whipped cream.
Serves 4

Blackcurrants and Redcurrants in Cointreau

Macerating (or soaking) the fruit in a Cointreau-flavoured syrup softens its texture and improves the flavour – so prepare this delicious fruit salad the day before you intend to serve it.

grated rind and juice of 1 orange
2 tablespoons clear honey
3 tablespoons Cointreau
250 g (8 oz) red-currants
250 g (8 oz) black-currants

Mix together the orange rind and juice, honey and Cointreau. Place the redcurrants and blackcurrants in a serving bowl, pour over the orange-flavoured syrup and chill in the refrigerator overnight.

Serve with whipped cream.
Serves 4

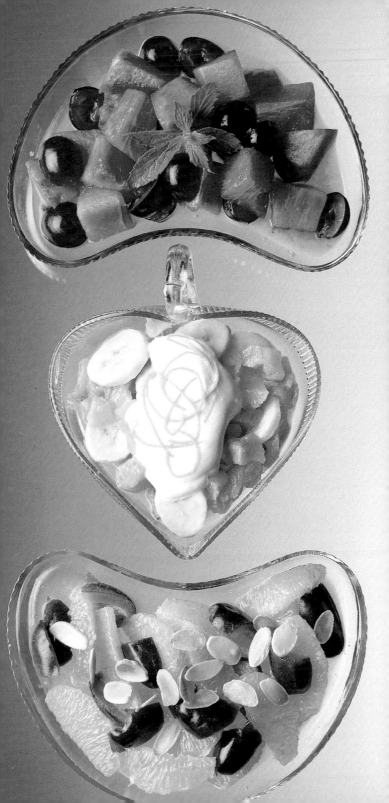

Watermelon and Grape Compote

1 small watermelon
250 g (8 oz) black grapes, halved and seeded
juice of 1 lemon
2 tablespoons clear honey
3–4 tablespoons orange Curaçao
mint sprigs to decorate

Cut the watermelon into quarters. Cut out the flesh, discard the seeds and cut the watermelon into cubes. Place in a bowl with the grapes.

Mix together the lemon juice, honey and Curaçao. Pour over the fruit and leave for 1 hour, stirring occasionally.

Spoon the fruit into individual glass dishes, pour over the juice and decorate with mint sprigs to serve.
Serves 6

Apricot and Orange Cream

250 g (8 oz) dried apricots, roughly chopped
300 ml (½ pint) orange juice
2 bananas
2 tablespoons Grand Marnier
1 orange
142 ml (5 fl oz) double cream
2 teaspoons clear honey
150 g (5.2 oz) natural yogurt

Place the apricots and orange juice in a bowl and leave to soak overnight.

Slice the bananas and add to the bowl with the Grand Marnier. Mix well, then transfer to a glass bowl.

Using a potato peeler, take the rind off half the orange, cut into fine strips and set aside. Grate the remaining rind and mix with the juice of half the orange. Stir this into the cream with the honey, then whip until it stands in stiff peaks. Stir in the yogurt.

Spoon over the fruit and sprinkle with the orange rind strips to serve.
Serves 6

Date and Orange Salad

4 oranges
175 g (6 oz) fresh dates, halved and stoned
2 tablespoons Cointreau
15 g (½ oz) flaked almonds, toasted

Peel the oranges, removing all pith, and break into segments over a bowl to catch the juice. Place in the bowl with the dates and Cointreau and mix together. Sprinkle with the almonds to serve.
Serves 4

Fresh Fruit Salad

2 tablespoons clear
  honey
120 ml (4 fl oz)
  water
thinly pared rind and
  juice of 1 lemon
1 red dessert apple,
  quartered and cored
1 pear, quartered and
  cored
1 banana
1 small pineapple
2 oranges
125 g (4 oz) black
  grapes, halved and
  seeded
125 g (4 oz)
  strawberries, sliced

Place the honey, water and lemon
rind in a small pan. Bring to the boil,
simmer for 2 minutes, then strain and
leave to cool. Stir in the lemon juice.

Slice the apple, pear and banana
into a bowl, pour over the lemon
syrup and stir to coat the fruit
completely.

Peel the pineapple with a sharp
knife and cut the flesh into sections,
discarding the central core.

Peel the oranges, removing all pith,
and divide into segments. Add to the
bowl with the pineapple, grapes and
strawberries and mix well.

Turn into a glass dish and chill until
required. Serve with whipped cream.
Serves 8

Melon Jelly Salad

1 large Ogen melon,
  halved and seeded
250 g (8 oz) black
  grapes, halved and
  seeded
2 kiwi fruit, peeled
  and thinly sliced
150 ml (¼ pint)
  water
50 g (2 oz) caster
  sugar
thinly pared rind and
  juice of 1 lemon
25 g (1 oz) gelatine,
  soaked in
  6 tablespoons cold
  water
150 ml (¼ pint)
  white wine
142 ml (5 fl oz)
  double cream,
  whipped

Scoop the flesh from the melon halves
with a melon baller, or cut into cubes,
and place in a bowl with the grapes
and kiwi fruit.

Put the water, sugar and lemon
rind in a pan and heat gently to
dissolve the sugar. Simmer for
5 minutes, then add the soaked
gelatine and stir until dissolved.
Leave to cool, then add the lemon
juice and wine. Strain into the bowl
of fruit.

Pour into individual glasses and
chill until set. Decorate with the
whipped cream to serve, or serve the
cream separately.
Serves 4

INDEX